50 Bedtime Bible Stories

B&H KIDS

Nashville, Tennessee

A Wonderful World

In the beginning, there was nothing at all: no sunshine, no land, no animals, no people. Can you even imagine that? Absolutely nothing!

Then God created heaven and earth. He made light so there could be day and night. He separated the water from dry land and covered the land with beautiful plants and trees and lovely green grass. He made the sun to shine during the day and the moon and stars to light the night sky.

God filled the seas with enormous whales and shiny fish, leaping dolphins and wobbly jellyfish. Then He filled the skies with beautiful birds of every color imaginable. Next He made animals of all shapes and sizes—spotted cheetahs that could run like the wind, slow tortoises carrying their homes on their backs, huge elephants with long trunks, and many, many more.

Last of all, God made man and woman and told them to take care of this wonderful world and all the living creatures on it.

God was pleased with all He had made and done. So on the seventh day, He rested and made that day a special day, a day to stop working and to give thanks.

Disobeying God

God had made Adam, the very first man, in His own image. He created a beautiful garden for him filled with colorful plants and wonderful trees, and told Adam to help himself to any fruit except for the fruit from the Tree of Knowledge. There were plenty of other delicious things to eat!

God brought all the animals and birds to Adam for him to name. But none of the animals were like him, and Adam was lonely, so God created a woman, Eve, to be Adam's special friend and companion. Adam and Eve had no clothes to wear, but that didn't bother them at all.

Of all the animals, the most cunning was the snake. One day, he said to Eve, "Did God really say you can't eat from the Tree of Knowledge?" The fruit looked so good that Eve picked some and offered it to Adam too, and they both ate it. At once, they realized they were naked and tried to cover themselves with leaves.

God was very angry. He cursed the snake and sent Adam and Eve away. From now on they would have to work hard to make their own food and clothes. Then He placed an angel with a flaming sword to guard the entrance to the garden.

Cain and Abel

Adam and Eve had two sons. Cain was a farmer who worked in the fields, and Abel was a shepherd. One day Cain and Abel both brought offerings to God. Abel brought the very best meat he could, and God was pleased. But God was not so pleased with the crops that Cain had brought.

Cain was so jealous of his brother that he went into the fields and killed Abel in a fit of anger. When God asked where Abel was, Cain answered rudely, "How should I know? Am I my brother's keeper?"

But God saw Abel's blood on the ground and was angry. He punished Cain and sent him far away from his home and family.

Noah Builds an Ark

Years passed, and soon there were lots of people in the world. But they were becoming more and more wicked, and this made God sad. He decided to send a terrible flood to destroy everything.

But there was one good man who loved and obeyed God. His name was Noah. God told Noah to build an enormous boat—an ark—so that he and his family might be saved along with two of every living creature.

People thought Noah was silly building a boat in the middle of the land, and they made fun of him. But Noah ignored them, for he trusted God.

It took Noah and his three sons a long, long time to build the ark. When it was finished, Noah, his wife, his sons, and their wives loaded the ark with food for themselves and the animals. Then God sent the animals to the ark, two by two, one male and one female of every kind of animal and bird that lived upon the earth or flew in the skies.

Once they were all safely in, God closed the door behind them.

The Flood

Now it began to rain—and oh, how it rained! Water poured down from the skies and covered all the land. Every living creature drowned. All the towns and cities were washed away. But the ark and its precious cargo floated free on a world of water.

For forty days and forty nights it rained. Then, at last, it stopped! After a while, the flood waters began to go down. Noah sent out a dove, and when it returned with an olive leaf in its beak, Noah knew that the flood was over, for the trees were growing again.

It was time for Noah and the animals to leave the ark. Noah was filled with gratitude. God promised to never again send such a dreadful flood. He put a beautiful rainbow in the sky to remind everyone of this promise.

The Tower of Babel

At first the world had only one language, so everyone could understand everyone else. There came a time when some of Noah's descendants decided to build a city that would be famous throughout the land and have a tower reaching to the heavens.

But God feared the people building the tower were becoming too proud and vain, so He made them unable to understand one other. Soon a great babble of voices was heard, with everyone speaking in a different language. No one could understand anyone else!

In all the confusion, the people stopped building and scattered far and wide. The tower became known as the Tower of Babel.

The Wonderful Coat

Jacob lived in Canaan. He had twelve sons, but Joseph was his favorite. To show just how much he loved Joseph, Jacob gave him a wonderful coat of many colors.

Joseph's brothers were jealous, but what really angered them was when Joseph began telling them about his dreams.

"Last night I dreamt we were collecting sheaves of grain when suddenly my sheaf stood up straight and yours all bowed down before it," Joseph told his brothers.

"What are you saying?" they growled. "That you're going to rule over us someday? Go away!"

Joseph dreamt that the sun, moon, and eleven stars were bowing down before him. Even his father was angry when he heard about the latest dream.

"You think your mother and I and your brothers are going to bow down to you? Don't get too big for your boots!"

But Jacob did secretly wonder what Joseph's dream might mean.

Sold into Slavery

Joseph's brothers had had enough. The time had come to get rid of their annoying brother! So one day when they were out in the fields, the brothers tore off Joseph's precious multi-colored coat and threw him into a deep pit. The brothers would have left him there, but soon they saw a caravan of Ishmaelite traders passing by on their way to Egypt. Quick as a flash the brothers decided to sell Joseph to the traders. They told his poor father that he had been killed by a wild animal!

In Egypt, Joseph was sold to one of Pharaoh's officials, a man named Potiphar. Joseph was clever and hardworking, and soon Potiphar placed him in charge of his whole household. But Potiphar's wife told lies about Joseph to her husband, and poor Joseph found himself thrown into jail!

There Joseph came across Pharaoh's wine steward and his chief baker, who had angered Pharaoh. They both had strange dreams and, with the help of God, Joseph was able to explain what the dreams meant. The baker had a dream about birds eating bread from his basket, and Joseph sadly told him that Pharaoh would order his execution, but the wine steward's dream about squeezing grapes into Pharaoh's wine cup meant that he would be pardoned. Joseph asked the wine steward to remember how Joseph had helped him, but when the wine steward was released from jail, he didn't remember!

Pharaoh's Strange Dream

One night, Pharaoh, the king of Egypt, had a strange dream. He was standing by the Nile when out of the river came seven fat, healthy-looking cows followed by seven more cows that were ugly and thin. They ate up the fat cows and looked just as sickly as before! Pharaoh had another dream. In this dream, seven thin heads of grain swallowed up seven healthy, full heads!

In the morning, Pharaoh sent for all the wise men of Egypt, but no one could tell him what his strange dreams might mean. Then the wine steward remembered Joseph, and the slave was brought before Pharaoh.

God helped Joseph explain the dreams. Joseph told Pharaoh, "The two dreams are one and the same. The seven cows and the seven heads of grain are seven years. The land will be blessed with seven years of healthy crops and fine harvests, but they will be followed by seven years of dreadful famine. You will need to plan very carefully to prepare."

Then Pharaoh replied, "Clearly you are the man for the job! I will put you in charge of my land, and you will be second only to me in all of Egypt!"

So Joseph traveled throughout the land to make sure food was put aside for the hard times ahead. Just as he had foretold, for seven years the crops grew better than ever before, and so much grain was put away in storehouses that he gave up counting it! After seven years, the famine began. When people began to run out of food, Joseph opened up the storehouses and sold the corn. No one in Egypt went hungry.

The Brothers Come to Egypt

The famine was bad in Canaan, too, and Jacob and his sons didn't have enough to eat. Jacob sent Joseph's brothers to Egypt to buy grain. Only the youngest brother, Benjamin, stayed behind. The brothers were brought before Joseph. With his golden chain and fine clothes, they did not recognize him and bowed down before him. Joseph couldn't help but remember the dreams he had had so long ago!

Joseph wanted to see if his brothers had changed, and so he decided to test them. First he told them to come back with Benjamin. Then, when they did, he sent them off with sacks full of corn, but before they went he hid a silver cup in Benjamin's sack!

The brothers were traveling home when guards came and dragged them back to the palace.

When the cup was found in Benjamin's sack, all the other brothers fell to their knees and begged Joseph to punish any of them, but not Benjamin, for his father's heart would break!

At this, Joseph knew that his brothers really had changed. He hugged them and told them who he really was. "Don't feel bad," he said. "God sent me to rule in Egypt so you wouldn't starve!"

The brothers were overjoyed. They rushed back to tell their father the good news, and Jacob gathered up his belongings, his herds and flocks, and he and all his family traveled to Egypt. Joseph came to meet him, and father and son were joyfully reunited!

The Baby in the Reeds

What could Moses' mother do? Her baby boy was healthy and beautiful, but the ruler of Egypt had ordered all Hebrew baby boys killed! So she wrapped baby Moses in a shawl, placed him in a basket, and lowered it into the water among the reeds.

That day, the king's daughter came down to the river and found the basket. "This must be one of the

Hebrew babies," she said, and she picked him up and cradled him gently.

Moses' sister was watching from behind some bushes. She bravely stepped forward and offered to fetch someone to nurse the baby. The princess agreed, and Miriam darted off to find her mother, who looked after Moses until he was old enough for the princess to take to the palace.

Plagues!

God sent Moses and his brother Aaron to ask the king of Egypt (Pharaoh) to let the Hebrews go free. But Pharaoh refused! So God sent a series of plagues upon the Egyptians, each more terrible than the last.

He changed the waters of the Nile into blood so that all the fish died. Then He sent a plague of frogs hopping into every nook and cranny. Gnats, flies, animal sickness, and boils all followed, one after the other, but still Pharaoh wouldn't change his mind!

Next came thunder and heavy hail that stripped the land while lightning struck again and again and fires blazed! Then came a swarm of locusts. Nothing green remained in all of Egypt. After this, God sent total darkness for three whole days.

But now the time had come for the most dreadful plague of all. . . .

The Passover

Moses warned Pharaoh that God would pass through the country at midnight and that every firstborn son in the land would die, from the son of Pharaoh himself to the son of the lowliest slave girl and even the firstborn of the animals as well! Pharaoh would not listen.

Moses told his people, the Israelites, that each family must kill a lamb, smear the blood on the door frame, and eat the meat in a special way.

The next day the land was filled with the sound of mourning, for all the firstborn sons had died, even Pharaoh's son. But God had passed over the houses of the Israelites, and they were spared!

Pharaoh finally agreed to let the Israelites free, and so Moses and his people prepared to leave Egypt.

Crossing the Red Sea

The Hebrews were terrified! They had traveled across the desert, but now their way was blocked by the Red Sea, and Pharaoh had changed his mind and had sent an army after them! "Why did you bring us all this way, just to have us killed or dragged back into slavery?" they cried to Moses.

But Moses did not give up his faith in God. "God will look after us," he said confidently. "And He will crush our enemy."

Then God told Moses to raise his staff and stretch out his hand over the sea to divide the water. Moses stood before the sea and raised his hand, and all that night the Lord drove the sea back with a strong wind and turned it into dry land. The waters were divided, and the Israelites went through the sea on dry ground, with a wall of water on their right and on their left!

The Egyptians were chasing after the Hebrews and swiftly followed them into the sea along the path that God had made. But God struck the Egyptians with confusion so that the wheels of the chariots came off and there was chaos. Then He closed the waters together, and the Egyptians were all swept under the sea! Of all that mighty army, there were no survivors—not one single horse, not one single soldier!

The people of Israel, safe on the far shore of the Red Sea, were filled with gratitude and relief and sang and danced in their joy, for they knew that their God was both mighty and merciful and they praised Him greatly.

Moses Sees the Promised Land

Moses and the Hebrew people spent many long hard years in the desert. They were hungry and thirsty, but God sent them food and water. He told Moses to go to Mount Sinai. There, on the top of the mountain, God spoke to Moses and gave him special instructions to pass on to his people, telling them how they should worship God and how they should live their lives. These were the Ten Commandments. The people promised to obey—but they didn't always remember!

When Moses was old, he asked God to choose someone to lead the people after his death. God chose Joshua, a good man.

Finally it was time for Moses to leave his people. He climbed a mountain, and God showed him the land of Canaan in the distance —the land that had been promised to his ancestors, a land of rich soil and flowing water, full of good things to eat and drink.

Moses died on the mountain. He was a hundred and twenty years old! The people were sad. They knew there would never be another prophet like Moses, who had spoken with God face to face.

The Walls of Jericho

It was time for the Israelites to take the Promised Land. The people of Jericho laughed at them from behind their strong, high walls. "You'll never get in!" they jeered. But Joshua was unafraid. He knew God would help them.

God told Joshua exactly what to do. Once a day for six days, the Israelite army marched quietly around the city while priests blew on trumpets. On the seventh day, when the trumpets sounded, the Israelites raised a mighty cry and the city walls trembled and then collapsed before them!

The Israelite soldiers charged in and took the city, and the story of how the Lord had helped Joshua take Jericho spread far and wide.

Faithful Ruth

Naomi was moving back to Bethlehem. Her husband and sons had died, and she wanted to go home. She begged her beloved daughters-in-law, Orpah and Ruth, to stay behind, for Naomi was penniless and she knew that her life would be hard.

Orpah and Ruth loved Naomi dearly and did not want to stay behind, but finally Orpah agreed to go home. Loyal Ruth, however, said earnestly to Naomi, "Don't ask me to leave! I will go wherever you go. Your people will be my people and your God will be my God!"

So it was that Ruth and Naomi came to Bethlehem. Soon they had no food left, and brave Ruth went out into the fields where workers were harvesting the crops and asked the owner, Boaz, if she could pick up any of the barley that his workers left behind.

Boaz had heard about how loyal Ruth had been to Naomi. He let her work in his fields and told his servants to share their food with her. He even told them to drop some of the barley for her to pick up!

When Ruth returned with a full basket of food and said how kind Boaz had been, Naomi knew that the Lord was looking after them, for Boaz was a relation of hers.

In time, Ruth married Boaz, and when they had a son, there was no happier woman than Naomi in all of Bethlehem!

Samson the Strong

Samson was stronger and braver than any other man! When he was born, God told his parents that he would deliver the Israelites from the Philistines. To show how special he was, Samson's parents never once cut his hair!

The Philistines feared Samson, for he carried out many attacks against them. But when he fell in love with the beautiful Philistine Delilah, she tried to find out the secret of his strength. Night after night, treacherous Delilah pleaded with Samson to tell her his secret. In the end he said, "If anyone were to cut my hair off, then I would lose all my strength."

That night the Philistines crept into his room and cut off his hair. He was powerless as they bound and blinded him and threw him into prison!

Over time, Samson's hair grew back. One day, the Palestinian rulers were gathered for a feast in a crowded temple. Samson was brought out to be made fun of. He was chained between the two central pillars of the temple. There he prayed to God with all his heart, "Give me strength just one more time, Lord, so I can take revenge upon my enemies!"

Once more, Samson was filled with strength. He pushed against the pillars with all his might, and they toppled and made the temple crash down, killing everyone inside!

A Stone in a Sling

David was just a shepherd boy. He was the youngest of his family, and he had many brothers who were older and stronger than he was. But God had chosen him as the future leader of Israel! The Israelites were at war with the Philistines, and the two armies had gathered to do battle. Young David had brought food to his brothers who were fighting in the army.

The Philistines had a mighty champion. His name was Goliath and he was powerful and strong—and almost ten feet tall! Goliath challenged the Israelites to single combat, but no one dared to fight him. No one, that is, but David!

David stood before Goliath. God had been with him when he had protected his sheep from lions and bears, and David knew that God

would be with him now. He stood there with nothing but his staff, a sling, and five stones. . . .

Goliath laughed at him, but David fearlessly ran forward, putting a stone in his sling and flinging it with all his might. The stone hit Goliath on his forehead. When the giant soldier fell to the ground, David raced up and cut off his head using Goliath's own sword. The Philistines were so shocked that they turned and ran away! God had helped a shepherd boy win the battle!

A Wise Ruler

Solomon was David's son. When David died an old man, Solomon was crowned king. Soon after, God spoke to him in a dream and told Solomon He would give him whatever he asked for.

Solomon thought carefully. Then, instead of asking for wealth or long life or great victories, he asked for wisdom to rule wisely over God's people, for he wanted to be a good king like his father.

God was pleased with Solomon's answer. "I will give you wisdom," God said. "But I will also give you those things you didn't ask for!"

When Solomon awoke, he felt comforted and strengthened, knowing that God was with him.

Two women came before Solomon holding a baby between them. They had both had babies at the same time, and one of the babies had died. Now each woman said this baby was her own!

The king called for a sword and then told a guard, "Cut the child in two, and give half to one woman and half to the other."

One woman cried out in horror, "No! No, my lord! Give her the baby! Don't kill him! I would rather she looked after him than he died!" But the other woman nodded, for she thought this was fair.

Then Solomon said, "Give the baby to the first woman. Do not kill him; she is his true mother."

Then people realized how wise and clever God had made Solomon.

Jonah and the Big Fish

Jonah was a prophet. One day God told him to go to Nineveh, many miles away, and tell the people there that unless they turned from their wicked ways, God would destroy their city.

Now Jonah did not want to go and warn the people of Nineveh. He thought they deserved to be punished! So instead of doing as God had told him, Jonah boarded a ship heading in the opposite direction of Nineveh!

A dreadful storm sprang up from nowhere. The winds howled, and the waves towered above the ship. Jonah knew it was all because of him. He had made God angry. So he told the terrified sailors to cast him overboard, and reluctantly they lowered him over the side.

Instantly, the sea became calm! The amazed sailors began to pray to God with all their hearts, realizing now that He was the one true God.

But what about Jonah? He sank swiftly to the bottom of the sea, certain he was going to die. But before he could take his last breath, God sent an enormous fish to swallow Jonah whole, and there inside the fish Jonah could breathe once again and was safe.

For three days and nights, Jonah sat inside the belly of the fish. He had plenty of time to feel sorry for having disobeyed God. He prayed to God, thanking God for saving him and letting God know how sorry he was.

Then God commanded the fish to spit Jonah up, safe and sound, onto dry land. And when God once again asked Jonah to take His message to Nineveh, Jonah was ready to do as he was told!

In the Lions' Den

Daniel had an important job in the court of King Darius of Persia. Daniel was an exile from Jerusalem, but the king trusted him. The other officials were jealous. They knew Daniel prayed every day, and they came up with a nasty plan.

The officials had the king sign an order stating that anyone asking anything of any god or man except the king should be thrown into a den of lions!

Daniel prayed just as he had always done. He would not stop or even hide what he was doing. His enemies rushed to the king and told him. Darius's heart sank, but he could not change the law.

"You have been loyal to your God. I hope He can save you," Darius said sadly as Daniel was thrown into a pit full of lions!

That evening the king did not sleep a wink. At first light, he rushed to the pit. "Daniel!" he cried out, more in desperation than hope. "Has your God been able to save you?"

How thrilled and amazed Darius was when he saw Daniel sitting among the lions, completely unharmed. God had sent an angel to shut the mouths of the lions! "Your God truly is wonderful!" said King Darius, and he ordered that from then on, everyone in the kingdom should respect and honor Daniel's God!

As for the wicked men who had tricked Daniel, they were thrown into the pit themselves, and this time the lions were ruthless!

The Brave Queen

King Xerxes of Persia was looking for a new queen. From all the beautiful young girls of the land, he chose lovely Esther. Esther did not tell him she was a Jew.

The king's advisor Haman hated Jews, especially Esther's cousin, Mordecai. Haman tricked the king into signing a decree that ordered the killing of all Jews. Esther's cousin told her that she had to try to get the king to change his mind.

Esther was frightened. To go before the king without being asked was punishable by death! Only if the king held out his scepter would the person be spared. But Mordecai sent another message, saying, "Maybe God made you queen precisely so that you can save His people."

Esther was scared but made up her mind to go to the king. When he saw her, he smiled and held out his golden scepter, asking her what she wanted.

Esther could not bring herself to ask the king there and then. Instead, she invited him and Haman to a banquet.

When the king came to dinner, he offered Esther anything she wanted—up to half his kingdom! Esther bravely told him that she was a Jew, and she asked him to save her people.

When the king found out how Haman had tricked him, he ordered Haman killed. The king couldn't change the decree, but he made another one saying that the Jews would be allowed to defend themselves.

When the Jews were attacked, they were able to fight back, and they overcame their enemies. They were saved! Every year the Jewish people celebrate the bravery of beautiful Queen Esther.

Mary Is Chosen by God

Mary lived in Galilee in a town called Nazareth. She was engaged to a carpenter named Joseph. One day, an angel appeared before her.

There were no empty rooms for guests, but Joseph and Mary finally found a place to spend the night. It was a room where the animals were kept.

There in Bethlehem, Mary's baby was born. She wrapped Him in strips of cloth and laid Him gently on clean straw in a manger.

Mary and Joseph looked down upon their son with joy. They named Him Jesus, just as the angel had said. God's own Son had been born into the world!

The Shepherds on the Hillside

That same night, some shepherds were keeping watch over their flocks in the hills above Bethlehem. Suddenly the sky was filled with a blinding light!

As the shepherds fell to the ground in fear, an angel spoke to them, "Do not be afraid. I bring you good news. Today, in the town of David, a Savior has been born to you; He is the Messiah, the Lord. Go and see for yourselves. You will find Him wrapped in cloths and lying in a manger."

Then the whole sky was filled with angels praising God!

When the angels had left, the shepherds looked at one another in amazement. They could hardly believe what had just happened! But they all knew one thing—they simply had to go to Bethlehem to see this baby with their own eyes!

The shepherds made sure that the sheep were safe and then hurried to Bethlehem as fast as they could. They made their way to the stable, and there they found the baby lying in the manger just as they had been told. Filled with wonder and awe, the shepherds fell to their knees before the tiny baby boy who would change the world forever.

Then they rushed off to tell everyone the wonderful news!

Following a Star

In a distant land, three wise men had been studying the stars. When they found a really bright star shining in the skies, they followed it all the way to Judea, for it was a sign that a great king had been born.

They asked King Herod in Jerusalem if he could show them the way to the baby who would be the King of the Jews. Herod was horrified! He didn't want another king around! His advisors told him of a prophecy that the new king would be born in the city of King David, in Bethlehem.

Then cunning King Herod sent the wise men to Bethlehem, saying, "Once you have found him, tell me where he is, so that I can visit him too!"

The wise men followed the star to Bethlehem, where they found baby Jesus in a humble house. There, they knelt before Him and presented Him with fine gifts of gold, sweet-smelling frankincense, and a spicy ointment called myrrh.

Then the wise men left to begin their long journey home. But they did not stop at Herod's palace, for God had warned them in a dream not to tell Herod where the baby was.

Water into Wine

As the years passed, Jesus grew to be filled with grace and wisdom. God loved Him, and so did everyone who knew Him.

When He was grown up, Jesus and some of His friends were invited to a wedding. Everyone was having a wonderful time—until the wine ran out! Jesus' mother Mary came to tell Him about the problem. She hoped He would help.

Several huge water jars stood nearby. Jesus told the servants to fill them with water and then pour the water into jugs and take them to the head waiter. When the head waiter tasted it, he was astonished. He exclaimed to the groom, "You have saved the best wine till last!" The jugs were filled with delicious wine!

This was the first of many miracles Jesus would perform.

The Amazing Meal

A huge crowd had gathered to listen to Jesus, and by evening everyone was very hungry. Jesus told His special friends, the disciples, to give the people something to eat. "But Master," they replied, "there are thousands of people, and we only have five loaves of bread and two fish!"

Jesus took the loaves and the fish and, looking up to heaven, broke them into pieces.

He gave the pieces to the disciples, who took them to the people and then came back for more. Jesus filled up the baskets again . . . and again . . . and again! There was enough bread and fish left in the baskets to feed the very last people! More than five thousand people were fed that day—with only five loaves of bread and two fish!

Calming the Storm

Jesus and His disciples were sailing across the lake. Jesus had fallen asleep. Suddenly, the skies darkened, rain poured down, and a fierce storm struck! Huge waves tossed the boat, and the disciples were terrified.

Jesus lay sleeping. The frightened disciples woke Him, begging Him to save them. Jesus looked up at them. "Why are you afraid? You have so little faith!" He said.

Then He stood up calmly, arms spread wide. Facing into the wind and rain, He commanded, "Be still!" At once the wind and waves died down and all was calm!

The disciples were amazed. "Even the winds and waves obey Him!" they said in awe.

Walking on Water

It was night, and waves tossed the boat violently. Jesus had gone ashore to pray, and the disciples were afraid. Then they saw a figure walking toward them on the water! They were scared until they heard the calm voice of Jesus, "It is I. Do not be afraid."

"Lord," said Simon Peter, "if it is You, tell me to come to You." When Jesus did so, Peter put first one foot then the other in the water and bravely stood up—on the water! But when he looked at the waves, his courage failed him, and he began to sink!

Jesus took Peter's hand, and together they walked to the boat. The wind died down, and the water became calm. "Truly You are the Son of God," said the disciples.

The Sower

Many people came to listen to Jesus. He wanted them to understand His message, so He told them stories. His stories, often called parables, let people think things through for themselves. To some they would just be stories, but others would understand the real message. . . .

Once Jesus told His followers a story about a farmer who sowed some seeds. The seeds all fell in different places: some fell on the path and were trampled on or eaten by birds; some fell on rocky ground where they withered because their roots could not reach the soil; some fell among weeds that choked them. Only those few seeds that fell on good soil grew into strong, healthy plants.

Jesus was saying that He is like the farmer and the seeds are like the message He brought from God. The seeds that fell on the path and were eaten by birds are like those people who hear the good news but pay no attention. Those seeds on rocky ground are like people who believe for a while, but when life gets difficult they give up easily—their faith doesn't have strong roots. The seeds that fell among weeds are like those who hear but let themselves become distracted and choked by other things.

But the seeds that fell on good soil are like those people who hear God's message and hold it in their heart. Their faith grows and grows!

The Weeds

Jesus told another parable: "Once a farmer sowed good seed in his field, but that night his enemy sowed weeds among the wheat. When the wheat began to grow, weeds grew too.

"His servants asked if they should pull up the weeds, but the farmer said, 'If you pull the weeds up, you may pull some of the wheat up too. Let both grow until harvest. Then we will burn the weeds and gather the wheat.'"

Jesus was talking about the end of time when everything that causes sin and all those people who do bad things will be weeded out of God's kingdom and destroyed. But the good people will be saved and will enter the kingdom of their Father!

The Rich Man and the Beggar

Jesus explained to His followers that they would find their reward in heaven, not on earth:

"There was once a rich man whose table was laid every day with fine food. At his gate lay a poor, hungry beggar named Lazarus, who used to long for the crumbs that fell from the rich man's table! But the rich man never thought about him.

"At last Lazarus died, and the angels carried him to Father Abraham's side, where he felt no more pain or hunger.

"Some time after, the rich man also died, but no angels came for him. He was sent to the place for wicked people. In torment he begged, 'Father Abraham, have pity and send Lazarus to dip his finger in water and cool my tongue, for I am so thirsty!'

"Abraham replied, 'Son, you received your good things on earth while Lazarus suffered, but now he is comforted here and you are in agony.'

"The rich man pleaded that his brothers might be warned, but Abraham told him the prophets had already given warnings. It would be their own fault if they didn't change their ways in time to avoid the same fate as the rich man!"

The Lost Son

Jesus told a story to explain how happy God was when sinners returned to Him:

"There was once a man with two sons. The younger one asked for his share of the property so he could go out into the world. He soon spent it all on enjoying himself. He ended up working for a farmer and was so hungry that sometimes he wished he could eat the food he was giving to the pigs!

"At last the son came to his senses and set off home to tell his father how sorry he was. 'I'm not worthy to be his son, but maybe he will let me work on the farm,' he hoped.

"When his father saw the son coming, he rushed out and threw his arms around him. The young man tried to tell him that he was not fit to be called his son, but his father told the servants to bring his finest robe for his son to wear and to kill the prize calf for a feast.

"The older son was outraged! He had worked hard for his father all this time, and nobody had ever held a feast for him! Yet here came his brother, having squandered all his money, and his father couldn't wait to kill the calf and welcome him home!

"'My son,' the father said, 'you are always with me, and all I have is yours. But celebrate with me now, for your brother was dead to me and is alive again; he was lost and is found!'"

The Good Samaritan

Once someone asked Jesus what the Law meant when it said we must love our neighbors as much as ourselves. "Who is my neighbor?" he asked. Jesus told him a story:

"A man was going from Jerusalem to Jericho when he was attacked by robbers. They stole everything before leaving the man by the road, half dead!

"Soon a priest passed by. When he saw the man, he crossed to the other side of the road and carried on his way. Then a Levite came along. He also hurried on his way without stopping.

"Nobody wanted to get involved—they were all too busy, too important, or too scared to help!

"Now, the next person to come along was a Samaritan. The Samaritans are not friends of the Jews, but when this traveler saw the man lying by the roadside, his heart was filled with pity.

The Samaritan carefully washed and bandaged the man's wounds before taking him on his donkey to an inn, where he gave the innkeeper money to look after the man until he was well."

Jesus looked at the man who had posed the question and asked who he thought had been a good neighbor to the injured man.

The man sheepishly replied, "The one who was kind to him."

Then Jesus told him, "Then go and be like him."

Jesus Enters Jerusalem

The city of Jerusalem was packed with people who had come to celebrate the Passover festival. It was also time for Jesus to start the last stage of His life on earth.

Jesus entered Jerusalem riding on a humble donkey. His followers threw their cloaks or large palm leaves on the dusty ground before Him, and He was met by an enormous crowd, for many had heard of the miracles He had performed. The religious leaders feared and hated Jesus, but many of the people truly saw Him as their King, and they tried to give Him a king's welcome, calling out "Hosanna to the Son of David! Blessed is the king who comes in the name of the Lord!"

But Jesus was sad, for He knew that soon these people cheering would turn against Him. They expected Him to fight with them against the Romans, and that was not what He was on earth to do.

The Lord's Supper

It was nearly time for the Passover feast, and a kind man had set aside a room for the disciples to prepare for it. That night, when they were eating, Jesus wrapped a towel around His waist, filled a basin with water, and then, kneeling on the floor, began to wash and dry the disciples' feet like a servant.

The disciples were speechless, but when Jesus knelt before Simon Peter, the disciple protested, "Lord, you mustn't wash my feet!"

Jesus replied gently, "You don't understand what I am doing, but later it will be clear to you." Jesus had washed their feet like a servant so that they could learn to do the same for one another.

But Jesus knew He would soon have to leave His friends. He was sad and troubled. "Soon, one of you will betray Me," He said. The disciples looked at one another in shock. When Judas Iscariot left the room soon after,

they didn't realize that he was the traitor and would tell Jesus' enemies where to find Him that same night—in exchange for thirty silver coins!

 Then Jesus handed them bread to represent His body and wine to represent His blood before telling them He would soon leave them.

Simon Peter cried out, "But Lord, why can't I follow You? I would gladly lay down my life for You!"

"Would you, My friend?" asked Jesus gently. "And yet you will disown Me three times before the rooster crows!" Peter was horrified. He didn't believe that could ever happen!

The Rooster Crows

Jesus had been praying quietly in the Garden of Gethsemane while His friends slept. Suddenly a crowd of armed people burst into the garden! At the head of them was Judas Iscariot. He had brought them there to arrest Jesus. Peter struck out with his sword, but Jesus stopped him. "I am the one you have come to find," Jesus said quietly. "Let these others go. You had no need to come here with swords and clubs."

When the disciples realized that Jesus was going to allow Himself to be taken prisoner, they fled in fear and despair.

Simon Peter followed the soldiers to a courtyard, where he waited miserably along with the guards warming themselves at the fire. One of the servants saw Peter and said, "Weren't you with Jesus?"

"No, you've got the wrong man!" Peter whispered, fearful of what might happen if the soldiers heard.

The servant shrugged but said to one of the guards, "Don't you think he looks like one of Jesus' followers?"

"I don't have anything to do with Him!" panicked Peter.

"You must be one of them," said one of the guards. "I can tell from your accent you're from Galilee."

"I swear I've never met Him!" cried Peter, just as a rooster crowed. Then Peter remembered what Jesus had said, and he wept in dismay.

It Is Finished

Jesus had been betrayed. He had been captured by Roman soldiers and sentenced to death. They had whipped Him, put a crown of thorns on His head, and made Him carry a heavy wooden cross up to the top of the hill. There they nailed His hands and feet to a cross and put up a sign saying, **'JESUS OF NAZARETH, KING OF THE JEWS.'**

As they raised the cross, Jesus cried, "Father, forgive them. They don't know what they are doing."

Two thieves were crucified beside Jesus. The first sneered at Him, but the other said, "Be quiet! We deserve our punishment, but this man has done nothing wrong." Then he turned to Jesus and said, "Please remember me when You come into Your kingdom," and Jesus promised the man would be with Him that day in Paradise.

The priests and Pharisees taunted Him. "If You come down from the cross now, we'll believe in You!" they mocked.

At midday, a shadow passed across the sun, and darkness fell. At three o'clock in the afternoon, Jesus cried out in a loud voice, "My God, why have You forsaken Me?" Then He gave a great cry, "It is finished!" and with these words, He gave up His spirit.

When the Roman soldiers felt the ground move beneath their feet and saw how Jesus passed away, they were deeply shaken. "Surely He was the Son of God!" whispered one in amazement.

Alive!

Jesus' body was placed in a tomb that was blocked by a large stone and guarded by soldiers. Mary Magdalene and some other women went to anoint the body. As they came near the tomb, the earth shook, the guards were thrown to the ground, and the women saw that the stone had been rolled away. And inside the tomb stood an angel!

The terrified women fell to their knees, but the angel said, "Why are you looking for the living among the dead? He is not here—He has risen!" So the women hurried away to tell the disciples the amazing news, but Mary Magdalene came back again later, alone.

As she wept, she heard footsteps, and a man asked, "Why are you crying? Who are you looking for?"

Thinking this must be the gardener, she begged, "Sir, if you have moved Him, please tell me where He is, and I will get Him."

The man only spoke her name, "Mary," but she recognized that clear, gentle voice! She gasped, and reached out, but Jesus said, "Do not hold on to me, for I have not yet ascended to my Father. Go and tell the others!"

So Mary rushed off with the wonderful news!

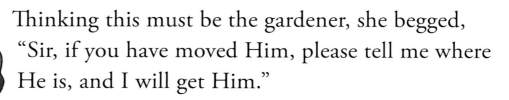

Thomas Doubts

That same evening, Jesus appeared to the disciples. At first, they couldn't believe it. Was He a ghost? But He spoke to them and reassured them.

However, Thomas was not there, and when they told him about it, he couldn't believe them, saying, "Unless I put my finger where the nails were, and touch the wound in His side, I will not believe."

A week later, Jesus came among the disciples again. Turning to Thomas, He said, "Put your finger in the wounds in My hands. Reach out and feel My side. Stop doubting and believe!" Thomas was overcome with joy!

Jesus said, "You only believed because you saw Me yourself. How blessed will people be who believe without even seeing!"

The Holy Spirit

Jesus had been taken up to heaven.
Before He left, He told His disciples,
"Stay here and wait for the gift that
My Father has promised you, for soon
you will be baptized with the Holy Spirit.
Then you must spread My message throughout the world."

Ten days later, the apostles were gathered together when suddenly the house was filled with the sound of a mighty wind coming from heaven. As they watched in wonder, tongues of fire seemed to rest on each person there! They were all filled with the Holy Spirit and began to speak in different languages—ones they had never spoken before or studied!

A huge crowd gathered outside. They were amazed when the apostles came out and began telling them all about Jesus in many different languages!

The Lame Man

A man sat begging outside the temple gates. He was lame and spent every day there, hoping for a spare coin or two. As the apostles Peter and John passed by, he looked up hopefully.

Peter stopped. "I don't have any money," he said to the lame man. "But I can give you something far better!"

As the lame man looked puzzled, Peter continued, "In the name of Jesus Christ, I order you to get up and walk!" To everyone's astonishment, Peter helped him stand up. The man took a cautious step, and then another, and then walked straight into the temple to give thanks to God!

Philip and the Ethiopian

Philip was a follower of Jesus. He was called by an angel to travel south on the desert road from Jerusalem. On his way, he came across a powerful man—the treasurer to the queen of Ethiopia. The man was traveling home in a fine carriage, and was reading from the Scriptures but couldn't understand what they said.

Philip was able to help the man. He sat beside him and explained the Scripture, which was about Jesus. Philip went on to tell him all the wonderful news about God's Son.

The Ethiopian man wanted to become a Christian right away, so Philip baptized him in a river by the roadside that very day!

Saul Sees the Light

Saul hated all the followers of Jesus! He was prepared to stop at nothing to stamp them out, and he thought he was doing what God wanted. Many believers fled to Damascus. Saul set off after them, but on the way, a blinding light suddenly flashed down from above! Saul fell to the ground, covering his eyes. A voice said, "Saul, why do you keep on persecuting Me?"

Saul began trembling. "Who are You, Lord?" he asked.

"I am Jesus," replied the voice. "Get up and go into the city, and you will be told what to do."

Saul struggled to his feet, but when he opened his eyes, he couldn't see a thing! His men led him into the city, where he prayed for three days without eating or drinking. Then God sent a disciple to him to lift the blindness.

Saul began to spread the good news about Jesus in the city. People were amazed. They could hardly believe it was the same man! But although his old enemies became his friends, his old friends soon became his enemies! Before long, they planned to kill Saul and guarded the gates to the city so that he could not escape. But the disciples lowered him in a basket over the city walls at night!

Soon Saul began to spread the good news all across the world.

A Sheet Full of Animals

One day when Peter was praying on the roof under the sun, he fell asleep and had a strange dream. In his dream, there hung before him a huge white sheet being lowered from heaven. It was filled with all sorts of animals, reptiles and birds—all creatures that Jews were forbidden to eat because they were considered unclean. Then Peter heard God's voice say, "Get up, Peter. Kill and eat."

Peter protested in horror, saying that he had never eaten anything unclean, but the voice replied, "Do not call anything impure that God has made clean."

God was telling Peter that His message was for all the people of the world, not just the Jews!

Taken for Gods

God spoke to Saul (who was now known by his Roman name, Paul) and told him that He wanted him to go on a long journey to spread the good news to people who had not yet heard about Jesus.

Along with his friend Barnabas, Paul traveled far and wide, speaking to everyone, not just the Jews, just as God had commanded. Sometimes Paul and Barnabas were welcomed, sometimes they were not!

In Lystra, in modern-day Turkey, Paul healed a lame man. The excited crowd believed that he and Barnabas were gods, and they wanted to offer them sacrifices and put wreaths around their necks! Barnabas and Paul had a hard job explaining to them that they were ordinary men and trying to tell them about God!

Shipwrecked

Paul was traveling on a ship to Rome but soon found himself in the middle of a dreadful storm! For days the ship was at the mercy of the sea. The passengers and crew were filled with terror, but Paul comforted them, for God had promised that they would all reach land alive.

Everyone was thrilled when the coastline came into sight, but then the ship struck a sandbar, and the surf began to tear the ship apart!

The centurion in charge ordered those who could swim to head for land, and he told the others to cling to pieces of the wreckage and float ashore. In this way, they reached land safely. Everyone on board was saved, just as God had promised!

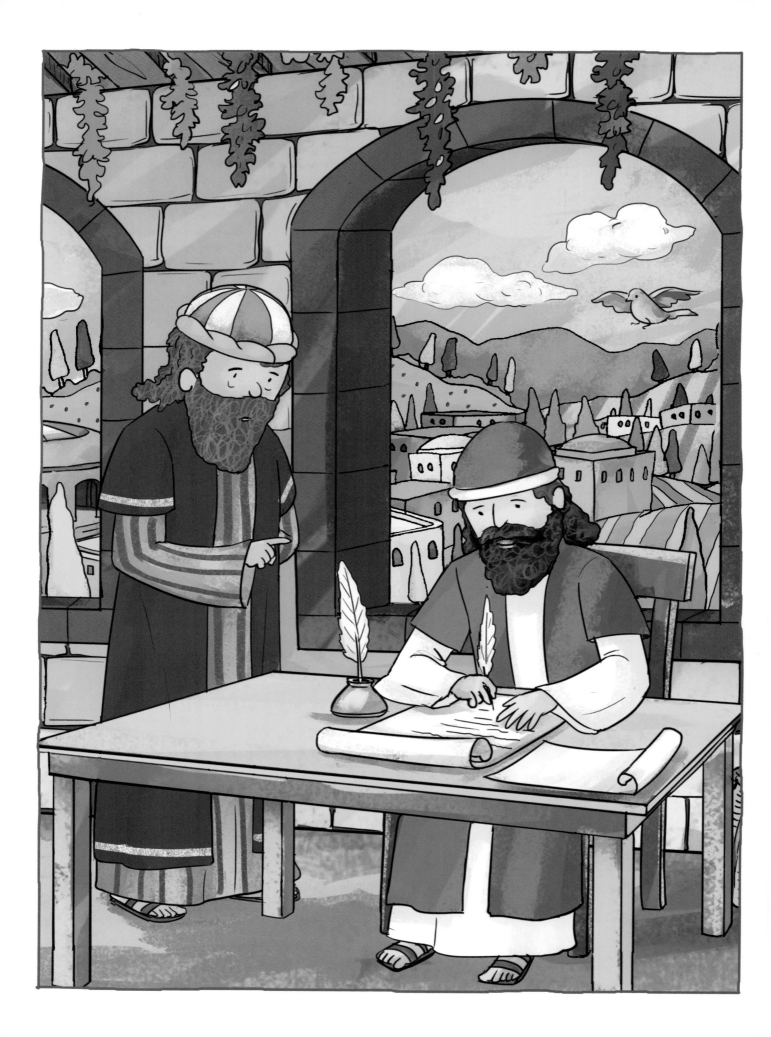

Rome at Last

Paul was a prisoner in Rome, but he was allowed to live by himself with a soldier to guard him. He had many visitors, and so he carried on telling people about Jesus. He also had time to write to his friends across the world, to encourage and help them as they set up new churches.

He told his friends to be patient, for their suffering would make them stronger and they would find their true reward in heaven. He warned them to trust in God and not to go back to their old ways, for Christ had set them free. He urged them to live good lives, filled with love and kindness, saying, "Three things will last forever—faith, hope, and love —and the greatest of these is love!"

Before Paul died, he wrote, "I have fought a good fight, I have finished the race, and I have kept the faith." Paul was God's faithful servant to the end of his days.